ANIMAL SENSE

ANIMAL SENSE

BY DIANE ACKERMAN

WITH ILLUSTRATIONS BY PETER SÍS

ALFRED A. KNOPF
NEW YORK

Hello!

A stapler with its tiny fangs
        cannot outwit
                orangutangs.

Rocks are very good at sitting,
        but never walk
                or take up knitting.

Living things all feel and sense
        their way through
                every happenstance. . . .

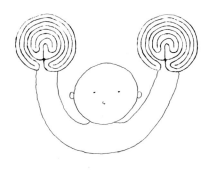

TOUCH

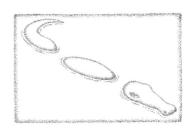

I

An alligator, for example,
has a skin chock-full of dimples
and puckers wrinkled like a blouse.
Do not invite one to your house.
He may grow cold and use his wiles
to con you with his fixèd smiles.

Never lend him your best sweater,
though he may sing an operetta
about being cold-blooded, or perform
a hula dance just to keep warm.

He knows a blanket of tiny marsh flowers
will keep him toasty, or he can bask for hours
on the riverbank with one leg dangling,
his tail in shade and his snout angling
up until he finds the perfect spot—
not too cold and not too hot.
I suppose he could carry the sun in a flask,
and he would if he could, but it's easier to bask.

II

Penguin babies,
on the other hand (or wing),
will cozy up to almost anything
summery and snug—
preferring Mom's tummy,
but a human hand or rug
also feels yummy.

Frantic for a big, smothery
featherbed cuddle,
they sometimes wobble around
in a chilly muddle,
gawking everywhere
for their next of kin.
"Hug me!" they squawk.
"I need wings to snooze in."

Then while the antarctic night
blusters and blows
and rainbow-bright auroras glow,
the air plunges to 40 below.
But penguin babies keep warm—
they peep songs of summer
and nuzzle in deep,
waltzing through their ice palace
on Mama's feet.

III

The real masters of touch
are not grabby monkeys
(who *do* love to clutch),
not turtles, who find a shell-scratch
sublime, not cockroaches,
whose belly-fingers can climb,
not snails (who have such
slimy sensitive feet),
not silky-pouched kangaroos,
mice, or jellyfish,
not leapsome gazelles
or lions acting kittenish,
not even animals
like squids that squish.

No, it's prairie dogs,
termites, anteaters, and such—
animals that dig for a living,
in darkness, through dirt,
and are constantly giving
pinches to some,
rubs and tweaks to others.
That's why the star-nosed mole
(who always wears a glove on his nose)
feels everything overmuch
and has dirty cheeks
but a dainty sense of touch.

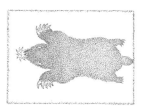

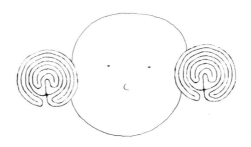

HEARING

I

Bats, when they are on the wing,
make a tiny, searching *ping!*
as they hurl their voices at the world
and listen for echoes straight or curled
that bounce off every living thing
(and dead things, too—a bike, a swing).

They spend their lives and a ton of bother
yelling at the bustling world and each other,
yelling at enemies, yelling at dinner,
yelling at loved ones, yelling at swimmers.

That's how they map the sky and earth,
and locate snacks and fill their girth
with luscious bugs both sweet and sour
(they can gobble up six hundred an hour!).

When they *ping!,* we hear nothing, nada, bupkus—
no complaint, bad temper, or loudmouthed ruckus,
nothing to signal that we've been yelled at—
how rude!—by a boisterous bat,

and it's just as well, because we couldn't hack it,
those rowdy dinner guests making a racket.
Yes, they're shouting at us as they dive and scutter,
but we don't hear so much as a mutter,
only moon-blessed quiet and the eeriest flutter.

II

Speaking in storm language,
humpback whales,
before they blow,
low rousing ballads
in the salad-krill sea,
and boom all the way
from Erb to Santa Cruz,
bog-low as a foghorn,
singing the blues.

And often they raise high
as angels' eyes
a refrain swoony as the tide
as they go a-caroling
beneath the galloping brine,
each whale singing
the same round runaway tune.

Dry fingers rub, drag,
drub a taut balloon.
Clicks and pops.
Dry fingers resume.
Ringing skeletal chimes,
they zing and rhyme,
then lung a long chant
done on ton tongues—

as, trapped below
the consciousness of air,
hungry or wooing
or lamenting slaughter,
jazzy or appalled,
they beat against
the wailing wall of water,
voices all in the marzipany murk,
they swim, invisible
but for their songs.

Sleek black musicians
playing their own pipes,
each body big as a meteorite,
they croon both at noon
and sprinkled by starlight,
glad to chain-rattle
and make ghostly moans,
roaming the world
like uneasy spirits,
a song in their bones.

III

Baby birds aren't born knowing their song.
They babble at first and just hum along,

learning to sing when they're downy and young
by listening hard, then rehearsing for fun.

Whistle a made-up tune, and before long
the baby birds will pipe out your new song.

It's pretty, no, when a whippoorwill throws
the boomerang of its voice across summer meadows?

Still, you could teach it a lullaby or simple *ding-dong,*
and it wouldn't question you or get the notes wrong.

A bird does not sing because it has an answer.
It sings because it has a song.

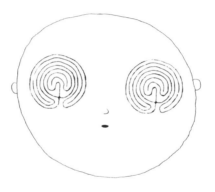

VISION

I

Bees hate the movies,
they loathe TV—
both appear slug-slow
to the eyes of a bee,
for whom the world zooms
in a whirlwind rush
of sun and nectar
and the occasional ambush.
But, man, can they dance!
Hips waggling, they say
in dance-talk: "What a banquet
over there, thataway.
Go left of the pond
and there's nectar galore.
Free lunch!"
Waggle, waggle.
"Tell Buzz and Seymour."

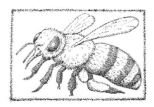

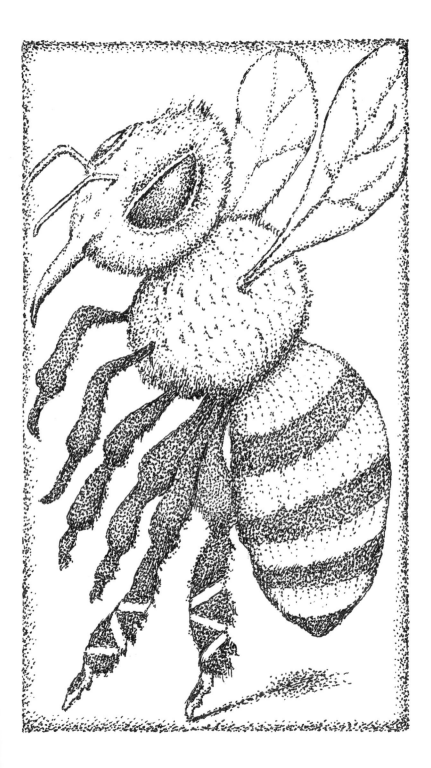

II

Consider the owl: a pair of binoculars with wings,
all eyes, giant eyes that swivel and swing
to spy tasty morsels with eye-gulps, and zoom
right down to feast in any old dining room,
big or small, provided there's scrumptulous food.
Then, wide-eyed and a bit impatient, he waits
for his guests to arrive—they seem awfully rude.
Why, they're whole minutes late. *Who* are?
He forgets. *Who who who?* Did he invite one or two?
Or did he invite a mob, an entire army?
For the feathered life of him, he can't remember *who*.
No matter, they're late. Perhaps they're lost
in a sandstorm or in a lagoon near Khartoum.
"I'd start without them," he thinks, eyeing the roast,
"if I could only remember *who who who*."

III

Swans are not white—they're clear.
The same is true of polar bears.
And blue jays are certainly not blue,
but also clear. Perhaps you knew.
In nature, colors aren't what they appear,
but subtle and tricky, and ever so quaint.
So, animal colors are rarely like paint.
Tiny air bubbles inside swan feathers
trap all the colors, splash them together,
and abracadabra! we *think* we see white there,
but as I said, swans are actually clear.
The same is true of polar bears.
And blue jays are certainly not blue,
but also clear. Perhaps you knew.

SMELL

I

Jackie, the German shepherd,
    out for a stroll, eagerly sniffs every curb, tree, and hole
        to discover what pooch pals were there and when,
            their health, age, mood, or latest yen.

Did Smitty pass by?
    Was he sad or frolicsome?
        For Jackie, it's like reading
            the gossip column.

The lane's full of invisible trails—
    odors loud as bells—
        and she adds her own scent
            to the patchwork of smells.

The next dog that comes along will read:
    "Jackie, 5:00 P.M., female, shepherd breed,
        cheerful, well-fed, and on the mend
            from a nasty little cold, seeks a friend."

II

"The enemy! The enemy!
Sound the alarm!
You're only seconds
from serious harm!"
a fleeing impala
signals with a snort
—not in words,
but in language of a smellier sort:

Waving its scented ankles
in the air, it leaps
high, wide, and sideways,
to skywrite a warning
certain to scare
all its impala pals—
a quick, fragrant "Beware!
Lions among us!
Run as fast as you can!"
the leaping impala smell-yells.
"Now scram!"

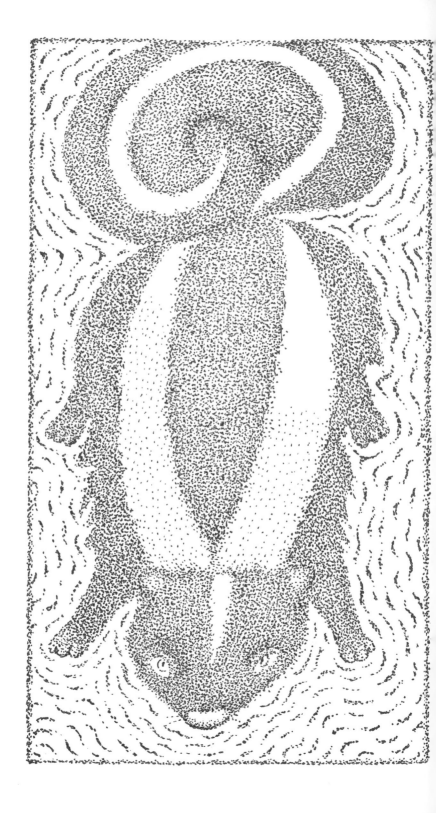

III

Smell as a weapon?
You've got to be joking.

"Oh, yeah?" says the skunk.
"You just keep provoking
me, and I'll spray you
with a smell
that's rotten and rancid
and scummy and beastly
and slimy and gruesome
and yucky and greasy
and sticky and ghoulish,
that burns like the dickens
and itches and sickens.
Then won't you feel foolish!

A smell that's bog-awful
and hard as a wrench.
Just try to chase me
off this garden bench,
and I'll do a handstand
and squirt you
with a horrible stench!"

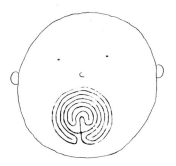

TASTE

I

Flies taste food with their feet.
If it's good to dance in, it's good to eat.

When one lands on a pile of cookies or plums,
he spits out a potion to dissolve the crumbs

into a sludge that's caramel-sweet,
where he sloshes, yumming the food with his feet.

Then he sucks it up through a long trunk disguised
like an elephant's (but shrunk to fly size),

and slurps it down in the blink of a bulging eye,
spits up again, eats again, and before he's done,

tramples everything into a gooey fly-pit of a slum.
Then he buzzes off in a well-fed delirium.

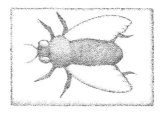

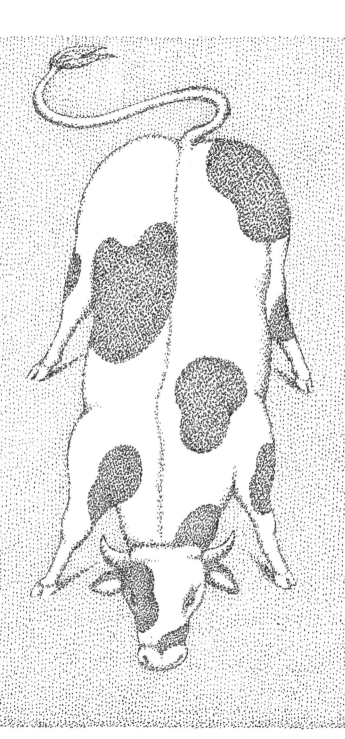

II

With plump rolling cheeks, a cow may be grazing
all the sunny day long, and what's truly amazing,
every meal is grass with a side order of grass,
plus huge dollops of grass smothered in grass,
followed by grass chops and, for dessert, more grass.

Yet her lolling-about tongue has taste buds all over,
even when she's young, thrice as many as ours.
Why? Think of all the treats *you* can taste: apple pie,
ice cream, pudding, fried chicken, sassafras...
Does a cow need more taste buds just to dine on grass?

Maybe she can taste every vitamin
and a hundred rare flavors we can't imagine:
new grass, dewy grass, grass missed by sun,
bluegrass, chop-suey grass, grass kissed by someone...
Otherwise she might be bored to tears
by her great green smorgasbord, steer clear

and never eat, if grass didn't taste exciting—
here a crazy lemon flavor, there a leaf sweet and biting.
"I'm feeling a little peckish," she might think.
"I'll munch a bunch of lunch and take a long drink.
Now, what am I in the mood for? Apples? Pizza? Bass?
No, something wild and wonderful... I know, I'll have grass!"

III

Sprawled alone along a branch,
the leopard lurks, awaiting lunch.
Her spots and claws, they have their uses
(and so do all her gastric juices).

But up there's the best place she can be,
lithe leopard in a tree,
because she can't run fast, you see.
Well, not for long. She just can't dash
after food that gallops past,
because her heart is far too small.
So the leopard stays arboreal.

Now down she pounces from her lair
to catch her prey quite unawares,
and quickly sinks her yellow teeth
into the tenderloin beneath.
Then she politely carries her meal upstairs.

DIANE ACKERMAN is the bestselling author of over twenty books of poetry and nonfiction, including *A Natural History of the Senses, Cultivating Delight*, and *Deep Play*, which was also illustrated by Peter Sís. She lives in Upstate New York.

PETER SÍS has written and illustrated numerous books for children, including *Starry Messenger* and *Tibet: Through the Red Box*, both of which were named Caldecott Honor Books. He lives in New York.

For all of earth's young animals, especially children
—D.A.

To Steve Heller
—P.S.

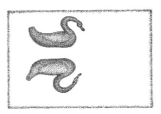

THIS IS A BORZOI BOOK PUBLISHED BY ALFRED A. KNOPF

Text copyright © 2003 by Diane Ackerman
Illustrations copyright © 2003 by Peter Sís

www.randomhouse.com

Library of Congress Cataloging-in-Publication Data
Ackerman, Diane.
Animal sense / by Diane Ackerman ; with illustrations by Peter Sís.—1st ed.
p. cm.
Summary: A collection of poems that tells how such animals as alligators,
bats, penguins, bumblebees, and skunks use their different senses.
1. Animals—Juvenile poetry. 2. Children's poetry, American. [1. Animals—
Poetry. 2. Senses and sensation—Poetry. 3. American poetry.] I. Sís, Peter,
ill. II. Title.
PS3551.C48 A84 2003
811'.54—dc21   2002075225
ISBN: 0-375-82384-0 (trade)
        0-375-92384-5 (lib. bdg.)

Printed in the United States of America
February 2003
10 9 8 7 6 5 4 3 2 1
First Edition